RECORD BREAKERS

MACHINES
AND INVENTIONS

DAVID JEFFERIS

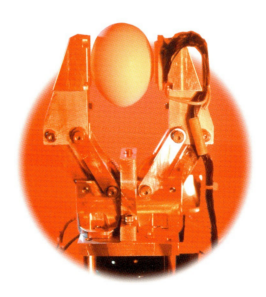

RAINTREE
STECK-VAUGHN
PUBLISHERS

A Harcourt Company

Austin   New York
www.raintreesteckvaughn.com

Copyright © 2003 Steck-Vaughn Company

All rights reserved. No part of this book may be reproduced or utilized in any form or by any means, electronic or mechanical, including photocopying, recording, or by any information storage and retrieval system, without permission in writing from the Publisher. Inquiries should be addressed to:
Copyright Permissions
Steck-Vaughn Company
P.O. Box 26015
Austin, TX 78755

Published by Raintree Steck-Vaughn Publishers, an imprint of Steck-Vaughn Company.

Library of Congress Cataloging-in-Publication Data is available upon request

ISBN 0-7398-6323-1

Acknowledgments
We wish to thank the following individuals and organizations for their assistance and for supplying material from their collections: Airbus Industrie, Alpha Archive, Apple Corp, BMW Group, Boeing Corp, Chrysler Corp, Deutsche Bahn AG, Dyson Ltd, Ecotech, Electrolux Group, Eurotunnel, Freedom Ship International Inc., Fujitsu Corp, Honda Motor Co Ltd, IBM Corp, Ron Jobson, Leicester City Museums, Museum of British Road Transport, NASA Space Agency, National Ignition Facility Project, National Space Centre, Nokia Corp, Panasonic Corp, ResidenSea Ltd, Sony Corp, SSC Programme Ltd, Toyota Corp, Transrapid International, U.S. Air Force, U.S. Marine Corps, U.S. Navy, Volkswagen AG, Ken Warby.

Diagrams by Gavin Page
Project modelling by Emily Stapleton-Jefferis
Educational advisor Julie Stapleton

We have checked the records in this book but new ones are often added.

Printed in Taiwan. Bound in the United States.

1 2 3 4 5 6 7 8 9 0 07 06 05 04 03 02

▲ The world's most expensive fighter jet is the *US F-22 Raptor*. There are plans for 295 of these jets to be built, at a cost of over $80 million each.

On the Cover: A robot arm delicately holds an egg.

CONTENTS

World of Machines	4
Ships and Subs	6
Trains	8
On Four Wheels	10
Flying Machines	12
Journey into Space	14
Communication Machines	16
Home Inventions	18
Computers	20
Robots	22
Power Machines	24
Machine Records	26
Machine Words	28
Machine Projects	30
Index	32

LOOK FOR THE TOOL SYMBOL
Look for the tools logo in boxes like this. Here you will find extra facts and records.

WORLD OF MACHINES

▲ The first steam engine was built by Thomas Newcomen in 1712. Before long, steam machines of all sorts were used everywhere, from factories to farms.

The way we live depends on machines, whether they are transportation machines, labor-saving gadgets in our homes, computers, cameras, or televisions.

The first machine was probably the wheel. We know that people in the Middle East, about 5,000 years ago, used donkeys to pull carts. About the same time the ancient Egyptians farmed with plows, while the Greeks and Romans later developed screws, gears, and pumps.

But the real machine age started only about 300 years ago. In the 1700s, inventors created hundreds of new machines, from steam trains to flush toilets.

◀ Automobile racing started not long after the car was invented in 1885. This car won the first official race in 1895. It traveled at a speed of 15 mph (24 km/h).

Before the machine age, most people spent their lives working to survive. The idea of a vacation was almost unknown. Today labor-saving gadgets in our homes and at work give us time for hobbies, vacations, and much more.

▶ This hand-operated wash tub was the latest home luxury 100 years ago.

Among the most recent inventions is the space rocket. Astronauts have already been to the Moon. There may be flights to distant planets in the future.

▲ The International Space Station is already the biggest machine in space. When fully assembled, it will be 356 feet (108.5 m) long.

⚒ EARLY MACHINES TIMELINE

3000 B.C. In Asia carts with wheels are used. Plows are used in Egypt.

100 B.C. A magnetic compass that points to the North Pole is invented in China.

1440s The printing press is perfected in Germany.

1500 A German locksmith, Peter Henlein, invents a clockwork pocket watch.

1590 A microscope was built by Zacharias Janssen of Holland. The telescope is developed in 1608.

1712 The first steam engine is built by Thomas Newcomen.

▼ One of today's top-selling music system is the Sony Walkman, first produced in 1979. Over 200 million have been made so far.

SHIPS AND SUBS

▲ Clippers were the fastest cargo sail ships of the 1800s. The record was 370 miles (596 km) sailed in one day.

There are hundreds of different kinds of ship, but they all fall into two main types, warships and commercial craft.

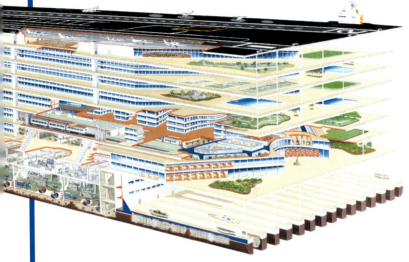

▲ The *Freedom Ship* is designed to hold parks, libraries, shops, and even a small electric railroad system.

The biggest ships today are oil-carrying supertankers, with the record being held by the *Jahre Viking*, which is 1,503 feet (458 m) long and weighs over half a million tons.

However, the *Jahre Viking* may be dwarfed by the *Freedom Ship*, if it is built. As planned, it will be almost 1 mile (1,317 m) long and will carry 115,000 passengers!

The *Freedom Ship* compared to a normal ocean liner.

🛠 BIG AND SMALL

1911 The *France II* is launched. At 417 feet (127 m) long, it is the biggest sailing ship ever built.

1991 The *Water Beatle*, the world's smallest submarine, is launched. The tiny craft is just 9.5 feet (2.95 m) long.

2001 *Adventure of the Seas,* the biggest cruise liner ever built, is 138,000 tons and can carry up to 3,114 passengers.

The most powerful warships are aircraft carriers and submarines. The first nuclear-powered carrier was the 1,102-foot (336-m)-long USS *Enterprise* of 1960. She was built to carry 5,500 crew and over 90 aircraft at speeds of up to 40 mph (65 km/h).

Below the waves, the russian *Typhoon* is the biggest submarine ever built, with a length of about 558 feet (170 m) and a 150-strong crew.

▲ A U.S. nuclear-powered aircraft carrier leaves port with a full load of planes on display. Once at sea, aircraft are parked below. The deck is used for takeoffs and landings.

▶ A typhoon sub weighs around 20,000 tons and carries a deadly load of missiles and torpedoes.

Small fins, called hydroplanes, move the sub up or down when underwater

Typhoon has two propellers and a single rudder

TRAINS

▲ The british *Mallard* is the fastest steam locomotive ever made. In 1938, the sleek machine pulled a seven-coach train at 42 mph (203 km/h).

Early railroad record-breakers were powered by steam engines. Today the fastest trains use clean and quiet electric motors.

The first trains running along metal tracks were built in the early 1800s. They were used to move coal in mines in Wales. But soon, inventors were building trains that could carry passengers. George Stephenson's *Rocket* of 1829 won a competition for reliability.

✴ FASTER AND FASTER!

1804 The first steam engine runs on a track in Wales.

1829 Englishman George Stephenson wins a railway competition with his steam engine, the *Rocket*. It travels at nearly 29 mph (47 km/h).

1893 The Empire State Express steam engine No. "999" goes over 100 mph (162 km/h) near New York.

1903 A German Siemens electric train hits 130.5 mph (210 km/h).

1964 The world's first regular train service to travel over 99 mph (160 km/h) is the Shinkansen express. It runs on Japan's Tokaido line.

1990 A French electric TGV train on a special run reaches 320 mph (515 km/h).

2001 Work begins on a Transrapid line in China. When the line opens, trains will complete the 18.5 mile (30 km) route in only seven minutes.

▼ Strong magnets allow the german Transrapid train to float just above a concrete track. It can go faster than normal trains with wheels.

Transrapid uses a wide concrete track

Record-breaking trains today have electric motors. The motor usually takes power from lines that run above the track. The TGV system in France has trains that run at 186 mph (300 km/h). The German Transrapid may become as popular: In 2003, a Transrapid line in China will open, reaching speeds above 310 mph (500 km/h).

▼ *Le Shuttle* electric engines carry cars and trucks through the Eurotunnel that links Britain and France under the English Channel. The freight cars are the world's biggest. They measure up to 13.5 feet (4.1 m) wide and 18.3 feet (5.6 m) high.

▲ Spain's ICE-3 trains give the fastest regular service in Europe. They travel at 218 mph (350 km/h) from Madrid to Barcelona.

metal arm gets power from overhead wires

ON FOUR WHEELS

▲ The Model T Ford was the first car to be made on a production line. From 1908 to 1927, nearly 790,000 "tin lizzies" were made each year.

▼ Three record-breaking cars. From left to right, a Volkswagen Beetle, a Toyota Corolla and a Mini.

The first car was built in 1885 by the German engineer Karl Benz. Today, millions of cars are made each year in factories all over the world.

The most successful cars have been ordinary but reliable. The top-seller is the Toyota Corolla, from Japan, with over 23 million being produced since 1966. In that time, hundreds of improvements have been made, and the body style has been changed nine times. The runner-up is the German Volkswagen Beetle, which was designed before World War II. It is still being made in Mexico.

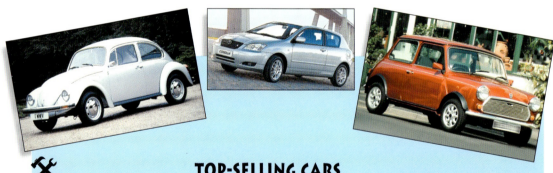

TOP-SELLING CARS

1885 Karl Benz builds the first car with a gas engine.

1908 The Model T Ford is the first car made on a production line. Over 16 million are made in all.

1937 The Volkswagen Beetle is designed, and has been made ever since. Over 21 million have been produced so far.

1959 The British Mini was the first space-efficient car. Its sideway-mounted engine allows seating for four.

1966 Toyota makes the Corolla. By 2001, it had become the best-selling car ever.

▶ The Land Speed Record (LSR) has been a challenge since the early days of the car. In 1997, the LSR was driven by British pilot Andy Green, who drove the jet-powered Thrust SSC to 763 mph (1227.985) km/h.

driver's cockpit

parachutes in the tail help slow the car down

jet engine on each side

metal roll bar protects driver and passenger in case the car flips over in a crash

▼ The Dodge Viper went on sale in 1991. At the time, it was the fastest U.S. sports car you could buy. It could speed up to 100 mph (162 km/h) and screech to a halt again in under 15 seconds. The latest models are even faster!

giant-sized engine

The extra-wide tires grip the road more.

FLYING MACHINES

▲ The pilot of the *Flyer* lay on the lower wing.

Aircraft have come a long way since the first flights of 1903. Today millions of people fly all over the world in jet airliners.

The first successful aircraft was the *Flyer*, built by Orville and Wilbur Wright in 1903. The Wright brothers made many flights, cruising at up to 30 mph (48 km/h). In the 1920s and 1930s, other pilots and planes opened up world air routes. The world of passenger jet travel began with the British Comet in 1952. Today, the busiest long-distance route is between the cities of New York and London. About 3.3 million passengers fly on this route every year.

two jet engines placed on each side of the cockpit

B-2 has a "flying wing" design, with no tailplane

◀ The batlike B-2 Spirit is the world's most expensive bomber. Each one costs about $1.3 billion! It is a "stealth" jet, designed to be almost invisible to enemy defenses.

There is a single-seat cabin in the nose section.

There is extra fuel carried in a tank on each side of the rocket

The rocket engine is in the tail section

⚒ FRONTIERS OF FLYING

1903 Orville Wright's first flight, on December 17. It lasts 12 seconds.

1909 Frenchman Louis Blériot flies across the English Channel, a distance of 23 miles (37 km).

1927 Charles Lindbergh mans first nonstop flight—34 hours—from the U.S. to France.

1939 First jet plane, the He 178, flies in Germany.

1976 Lockheed SR-71A becomes the fastest jet ever, at 2,193 mph (3,530 km/h).

1986 Dick Ruton and Jeana Yeager pilot *Voyager* in the first nonstop flight around the world.

▲ The X-15 rocket-plane still holds the record for the fastest crewed aircraft flight. In 1967, William Knight flew the X-15 at 4,522 mph (7277 km/h).

▶ The Airbus A380 will be the world's largest airliner when it goes into service in 2006. The huge jet, carrying up to 555 passengers, will sell for about $230 million.

JOURNEY INTO SPACE

◀ Crew of *Apollo 11*, the Moon-landing flight of 1969.

The first spacecraft was *Sputnik 1*, launched in 1957. Only 12 years later, humans landed on the Moon.

The *Saturn V* rocket was built for the Moon-landing missions of the 1960s and 1970s. It is the biggest spacecraft ever built. At launch, the huge rocket weighed 3,200 tons (2,903 tonnes) and stood 363 feet (110.6 m) high.

The three astronauts sat in a tiny command module (CM) at the top of the craft. This was the only part of the Apollo that would return to Earth.

◀▼ The *Saturn V* command module, left, had just enough room for three astronauts and their equipment.

command module was cone-shaped

command module landed in the sea after flight

▲ Today the Space Shuttle is the world's biggest crewed spacecraft. It is designed for a crew of up to seven. Here you can see a load in the big cargo bay.

Sputnik 1 had four radio antennas

🛠 LEAVING PLANET EARTH

1957 The first artificial satellite is launched. Russia's *Sputnik 1* weighs 185 pounds (84 kg) and is the size of a football.

1961 Russian cosmonaut Yuri Gagarin is the first human in space.

1969 Astronauts Neil Armstrong and Edwin "Buzz" Aldrin are the first humans on the Moon.

1971 Russia flies the first station in space. It is called *Salyut 1* and weighs nearly 20 tons.

1981 U.S. Space Shuttle's first flight.

1999 First section of the International Space Station (ISS) is placed in space by a Space Shuttle crew.

COMMUNICATION MACHINES

Communicating long distances was once a matter of sending a letter, then waiting for a reply. Today's electronic machines make this process almost instant.

▲ The Wheatstone telegraph was used in 1839 for a 13.5-mile (22-km) line.

◀ The first radio show was broadcast by the U.S. station KDKA in 1921. By 1930, there were thousands of stations around the world.

The ancestor of the today's Internet was the telegraph of the 19th century. The telegraph was as exciting then as the Internet is today. You could send a long-distance message along a telegraph wire in minutes, instead of days or weeks.

Television started in 1932, with broadcasts by the BBC in Great Britain.

▶ An early portable television from the 1950s was a big machine, since the equipment used was still very heavy and bulky.

plastic case   *metal frame*   *display screen*   *electronic parts*

antenna   *microphone*   *rechargeable batteries*

Mobile phones and the Internet have changed the way many of us live. Today most people have a computer in the home, so they can connect to the Internet easily. Mobile phones are even more popular. In Finland, 70 percent of adults have one or more mobile phones.

▲ Mobile phones are jam-packed with electronics. Many mobile phones can also link to the Internet.

🛠 INTERNET RECORDS

1969 An early form of Internet, the ARPAnet, is launched as a military communications system.

1972 U.S. computer programmer Ray Tomlinson devises first e-mail program.

1989 The World Wide Web is demonstrated.

1994 There are over 10,000 websites, and a pizza can be bought online.

1996 There are over 500,000 websites online.

2000 Internet advertising rises by almost half since 1999. Advertisers spent a record $2.9 billion.

2001 Several electronic companies create watches that can also play music from the Internet.

watch/music player weighs only 1.5 ounces (43g)

HOME INVENTIONS

▲ The first sewing machine was patented in 1851 by Isaac Merritt Singer. It was driven by pushing a foot pedal. By 1976, you could get an electronic sewing machine that could sew in 25 different stitch patterns.

In the past, homes had very few machines. Today, most houses are packed from top to bottom with high-tech gadgets.

Until the 20th century, lots of time was spent doing chores. There was a day for washing, a day for cleaning, and so on. What changed things was mains electricity (first available in 1882), which was a good source of power for many labor-saving gadgets in the home.

One early electric invention was the toaster. In 1905, an engineer named Albert Marsh made a wire, using a mixture of metals that glowed hot but did not break easily. Just a few years later, dozens of models of toaster were on sale.

◀ Electric washing machines were first made in the 1920s; before then, clothes were dried by rolling them in a hand wringer.

▶ The first spin dryer of 1957 weighed 661 pounds (300 kg). By 2001, the most powerful model weighed just 200 pounds (91 kg).

drum has 4,923 holes to get rid of water quickly

Internet screen is built into door of refrigerator

▲ This refrigerator was the first to have an Internet link. Food can be ordered when supplies run low.

Refrigerators were first sold in 1913, and big sales brought prices down: In 1920 one cost around $600; nine years later the price was less than half this. In 2001, an Internet-linked refrigerator cost around $7,250. Soon such a link could be included as standard.

✖ MAKING HOMES EASIER TO LOOK AFTER

1882 Inventor Thomas Edison starts the first electric power station in New York. It supplies 225 homes.

1913 First refrigerator is made for use in the home.

1929 First kitchen sink waste-disposal unit is developed by General Electric.

1932 First electric dishwasher goes on sale.

1947 First microwave cooker, named the "Radarange," goes on sale. Early ones are as big as a refrigerator.

1955 First home freezer goes on sale, with smaller versions available a few years later.

1980s Computer controls start to be included in most household appliances, making them cheaper and more reliable.

COMPUTERS

▲ The first computer was *Colossus*, built in 1943. It was made to break secret message codes in World War II.

Early computers were very big, but were no better than a modern pocket calculator. Today's computers are smaller, cheaper, and more powerful.

In 1943, the boss of the IBM company predicted that the world would need "maybe five computers." He might have been right if computers had stayed large, but their shrinking size and price have put them in every area of our lives. Experts think that there are now about 600 million computers worldwide!

▶ Most new computers break performance records. Apart from its regular computer functions, this 2001 laptop model plays music and video discs, and can edit home movies.

✖ ADVANCE OF THE COMPUTER

1943 *Colossus* code-cracking computer used in World War II. Also in 1943, work starts on the U.S. ENIAC. It uses a set of instructions, the ancestor of today's programs.

1954 General Electric is first company to use a computer, a Univac model.

1981 First personal computer is made by IBM.

1984 Apple Macintosh computer uses a point-and-click screen display, with a mouse. This helps make computers easier to use.

1993 Computers are used to make realistic-looking dinosaurs in the film *Jurassic Park*.

2000 *Super Mario Brothers* is the best-selling computer game, with over 40 million copies sold.

▲ Computers are in charge on the Space Shuttle. Landings are computer-controlled, all the way from space to the runway.

In aircraft and spacecraft, computers are used to show flight information in the cockpit. Video screens show speed, height, position, and other information. The equipment is far more reliable than the old-fashioned mechanical equipment that used dials and pointers to function.

▼ In 1997, the IBM *Deep Blue* computer was the first machine to beat a human in a series of chess games.

first chess programs were made for home computers in the 1980s

ROBOTS

▲ C3PO is one of the most famous sci-fi movie robots.

Robots used to be the stuff of sci-fi stories. Now they are made for real-life jobs.

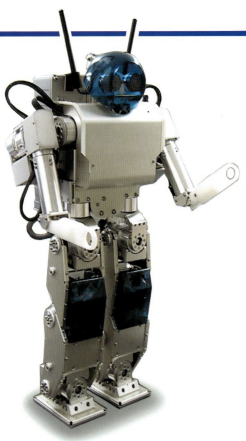
▲ The latest walking robot is the 19-inch (48-cm)-tall Fujitsu HOAP. It can be controlled by signals from a laptop computer.

For many years the word "robot" has been used for almost any machine that works by itself, without needing constant attention. For example, in car factories robot machines do precise jobs such as welding or painting.

In 1996, the Japanese Honda company built the P2 robot. It was the first humanlike robot that could walk properly without falling over.

Aibo-type robot dog barks, walks, and wags its tail

REIGN OF THE ROBOTS

1893 U.S. engineer George Moore makes a steam-powered "walking man" that can walk at 9 mph (14.5 km/h).

1948 U.S. researcher Dr. W. Grey Walter builds electronic robot "tortoises" that can go by themselves to a mains plug for a battery recharge.

1968 A small, wheeled robot named Shakey learns to find its way out of a maze.

1972 Unimation becomes the first company to make industrial robot equipment.

1996 The Honda P2 robot can go up and down stairs, and can keep its balance if pushed sideway. The P3 model of 1997 can also walk over obstacles.

2000 The popular Sony Aibo robot dog goes on sale. In a few minutes some 3,000 Aibos are sold, at $2,000 each.

▶ Metal parts of a car are welded together by an industrial robot. These machines do not have complete bodies. For this job, only an arm is needed.

▲ The Honda P2 had batteries that lasted just 20 minutes.

▲ In 1997 the first remote-controlled roving vehicle landed on the planet Mars. Future rovers, such as the one shown here, will be robots that can steer themselves around rocks and craters.

POWER MACHINES

viewing area

The race is on to find and use new sources of power before oil, gas, and coal reserves run out. And the cleaner these energy sources are, the better.

Many scientists agree that wind power is a good way to provide energy, since it produces no pollution. The giant wind turbine shown here is an Enercon E-66, claimed by its German makers to be the most efficient machine of its kind in the world.

The E-66 is huge, with three 101-foot (30.8-m)-long blades, yet it takes only a few days to assemble. This one produces enough electricity for about 3,000 people living in the town of Swaffham in England.

◄ Visitors climb 305 steps to a viewing area.

► On a clear day the view is fantastic.

🛠 MACHINES THAT MAKE CLEAN ENERGY

1981 World's largest wind farm is built in California with 6,000 turbines.

1993 British inventor Trevor Baylis devises a radio that uses clockwork for power instead of batteries.

1998 Wind power is the fastest-growing source of energy in the world.

2000 The biggest users of solar energy are Switzerland, Germany, and Japan.

2001 Most Israelis use solar-powered water heaters.

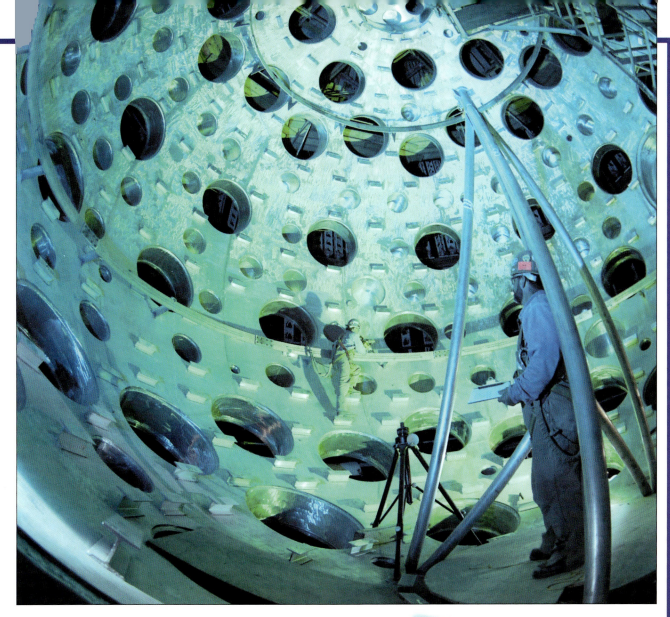

▲ Researchers check the huge research laser for a test. The beams will fire through the holes.

Scientists are trying another way to make clean energy, with this laser machine. It is the biggest of its kind in the world. A laser is a beam of light that can be made strong enough to burn through steel. The machine's 192 lasers will fire at a pellet of fuel to make energy hotter than the Sun!

▲ Over 20,000 of these clockwork-powered radios are made every month. One winding charges a battery for about 40 minutes.

MACHINE RECORDS

▲ The box camera was the first popular type of camera.

Here are some facts and records from the world of machines and inventions.

SAY CHEESE!
The very first photograph was taken in 1827 by Joseph Niépce from France. It was a very fuzzy view from a window in his home. In 1888, George Eastman produced the easy-to-use Kodak camera. To get prints you mailed the camera to Kodak. The firm removed the film, processed it, and then sent the prints back.

CLEVER INVENTOR
Thomas Edison (1847–1931) is considered the world's greatest inventor. He thought up or improved over 1,000 machines, including the phonograph, microphone, and light bulb.

MUSCLES IN FLIGHT
The first powered flight was by Orville Wright in 1903. However, it took until 1979 before a human-powered aircraft was successful. The first long flight was by U.S. cyclist Bryan Allen, who pedaled the *Gossamer Albatross* across the English Channel. The plane had a wingspan of nearly 95 feet (29 m), but weighed just 55 pounds (25 kg)!

BIG TELESCOPES
The biggest telescope in space is the Hubble Space Telescope (HST). It is as big as a school bus and has been taking pictures of stars and planets since 1990. On Earth, the Keck telescope in Hawaii is the biggest. Its light-collecting mirror is made of 36 hexagons that link up like a honeycomb.

◄ The first combat jet able to take off and land vertically is the Harrier. It was developed from the British experimental P1127, which first flew in October 1960.

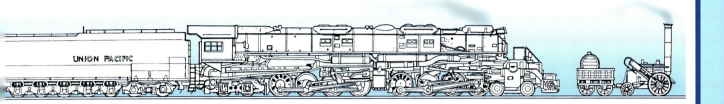

▲ The "Big Boy" locomotives were the biggest steam locomotives ever made, weighing over 550 tons. Big Boys could haul some 5,500 tons of freight.

KEEP WALKING!

Trevor Baylis, who invented the clockwork-powered radio and torch, has also devised shoes that generate electricity. In 2000, walking tests proved that they could supply enough power for a mobile phone.

CAR-CRAZY WORLD?

In the year 1900, there were about 50,000 motor vehicles worldwide. By 2000, there were over 650 million! The new vehicles are cleaner than the older models, so there is less pollution than in the 1960s.

GREAT GAME MACHINE

The best-selling computer game machine of 2000 was the Sony *Playstation 2* (PS2). In the first two days it was on sale, 980,000 PS2s were sold. But the *Game Boy* is also very successful—Nintendo has made 115 million so far.

FASTEST COMPUTER

In 2001, Compaq produced the Terascale, which became the world's fastest computer, able to perform 6 trillion (or 6,000,000,000,000) calculations per second.

ROBOT WORLD

Japan leads the world in using industrial robots. Worldwide, there are about 750,000 robots in factories, and Japan has more than half of them. Japanese robot researchers see a big future for robots, such as using them to help patients in hospitals as well as old people.

◀ The record for fastest speed reached on water is held by Ken Warby. In 1978, he raced to more than 318 mph (511 km/h). He now has a new boat (left) which could go even faster.

▲ The highest jet flight was by a Russian MiG-25 that achieved 23 miles (37,650 m) in 1977. Now you can buy a passenger flight aboard a MiG-25—but it costs about $12,000!

MACHINE WORDS

▲ This robot animal was featured online in 2001.

Here are some words used in this book that you may not know.

CLIPPER (KLIP-ur)
A type of sailing ship built for speed, before the days of steamships. Clippers raced in the 1800's, especially to carry tea from China to Europe.

E-MAIL (EE-mayl)
Short for electronic mail. The system that sends messages between computers, using the the Internet as the carrier.

INTERNET (IN-tur-net)
A system that links computers worldwide. Signals may pass along telephone wires, cables or by radio. The Internet also includes the World Wide Web, which shows information on websites, that fill a screen with words, pictures, and often sounds and movies.

▶ Laser beams can be seen here as colored straight lines.

LASER (LAY-zur)
A type of light beam that stays focused very tightly, rather than fanning out like the light from a torch.

NUCLEAR POWER (NOO-klee-ur POU-ur)
Type of energy that uses the very hot (and dangerous) metal uranium to boil water. The resulting steam can furnish electricity. Aircraft carriers and military submarines are two ships that use this form of power.

PHONOGRAPH (FOH-nuh-graf)
The earliest machine that could record sound, invented by Thomas Edison in 1877.

PRODUCTION LINE (pruh-DUHK-shuhn LINE)
A way of making cars (and other machines) using a slowly moving line, on which parts are added as the line progresses. A car usually starts with an empty metal body shell, to which seats, engine, wheels, and other parts are added. Many car factories produce hundreds of vehicles a day on production lines.

PROGRAM (PROH-gram)
A set of instructions that tells a computer to do a particular job. There are thousands of programs. For example, some are for word processing, graphics, or computer games.

ROBOT (ROH-BOT)

A machine that can do certain tasks without needing much attention. The word comes from the Czech "robota" which means "work." Science-fiction robots usually look something like metal people. One famous example is C3PO, the robot from the movie *Star Wars*.

SATELLITE (SAT-UH-LITE)

Any space object that circles around, or orbits another. It may be a natural satellite, such as the Earth's Moon, or a human-made, artificial one. Examples of these include the International Space Station (ISS) and Russian Sputniks.

SOLAR POWER (SOH-LUR POU-UR)

A machine that can extract the energy from sunlight. Some solar systems use the Sun's heat to warm water. Others are made of special materials that convert energy in light to electricity.

STEALTH (STEL-TH)

A military aircraft that is built to be nearly invisible to enemy detection systems.

TELEGRAPH (TEL-UH-GRAF)

A communications system that came before the telephone. It also used wires, but could send and receive only coded signals, not speech.

▲ Some mobile phones now use Internet links to show pictures as well as sound.

TGV

A special railway system that has been built across France. The letters "TGV" stand for *Train à Grande Vitesse*, or high-speed train.

VERTICAL (VER-TUH-KUHL)

Straight up or down.

WELDING (WELD-ING)

A method of joining metals together by melting them at the joining edges.

WIND TURBINE (WIND TUR-BINE)

Any modern machine that extracts energy from the wind. There are many different designs, but most of them use sails that look like aircraft propellers.

◄ This type of TGV train is called a Duplex. It has decks on two levels, a café and even a changing room for babies.

MACHINE PROJECTS

These experiments show you some simple machine science.

Microscopes have been around for more than 400 years. Today's optical equipment also includes telescopes and binoculars.

They are all based on the same idea. Glass lenses are used to bend light and give a magnified, or enlarged, image.

▲ A simple microscope gives young scientists a good start in their studies. The other tools are used to prepare specimens.

▶ These binoculars are small enough to carry in your pocket.

MAKE A WATER-DROP MICROSCOPE

This little machine uses the naturally curved shape of a water drop to bend light like the lens of a microscope. You can use it to magnify a printed picture and see the pattern of small printed dots that make up the image.

1. You need a card rectangle, a hole-puncher, modeling clay, a can, and a printed picture.

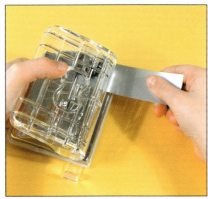

2. Line up the card in the hole puncher. Press out a hole in one end of the card.

30

REDUCING FRICTION

Oil is used in many machines to allow parts to slide easily against each other. A thin film of oil keeps them slightly apart, reducing the rubbing action called friction.

◀ Oil is used to keep car engines and many other moving parts working smoothly.

1. You need a screw-top jar and dishwashing liquid. Unscrew the top, then tighten it. Feel how your hand grips the lid.

2. Squeeze some of the liquid over the lid. Now try and open it. Your hand should slip, now that the friction is much less.

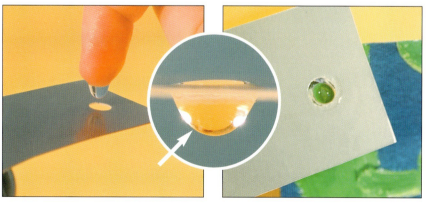

3. Lay the card on top of the can. Fix it firmly into place with the modeling clay.

4. Carefully place a drop of water in the hole. It should form the lens shape arrowed.

5. Hold the printed picture underneath the water drop and spot the dots.

INDEX

aircraft 2, 12-13, 21, 26, 27
Aldrin, Edwin "Buzz" 15
Allen, Bryan 26
Armstrong, Neil 15
ARPAnet 17

Baylis, Trevor 24, 27
Benz, Karl 10
Blériot, Louis 13

cars 4, 10–11, 22, 27, 28, 31
communication 16–17
Compaq computer 27
computers 17, 20–21, 27, 28

Eastman, George 26
Edison, Thomas 19, 26, 28
electricity 18, 27, 28

Gagarin, Yuri 15
General Electric 19, 20
Green, Andy 11

Henlein, Peter 5
household machines 18–19

IBM company 20, 21
International Space Station (ISS)
    5, 15, 29
Internet 16, 17, 19, 28, 29

Janssen, Zacharias 5

Knight, William 13
Kodak 26

Land Speed Record (LSR) 11
laser 25, 28
Lindbergh, Charles 13

Marsh, Albert 18
microscope 5, 30
microwave cooker 19
mobile phones 17, 27, 29
Moore, George 22

Newcomen, Thomas 4, 5
nuclear power 28

production line 10, 28

radio 16, 24, 25, 27, 28

robots 22–23, 27, 28, 29
Rutan, Dick 13

satellite 15, 29
ships 6-7, 27, 28
Singer, Isaac Merritt 18
solar energy 24, 29
spacecraft 5, 14–15, 21
stealth 12, 29
steam engines, machines 4, 5
Stephenson, George 8
submarines 6-7, 28

telegraph 16, 29
telescopes 5, 26
television 16
Tomlinson, Ray 17
trains 8–9, 27

Walter, Grey 22
Warby, Ken 27
welding 22, 29
wind power 24, 29
Wright, Orville 12, 13, 26
Wright, Wilbur 12

Yeager, Jeana 13

©Belitha Press Ltd. 2003